The Liturgy

and

Music

A Study of the Use of the Hymn
in Two Liturgical Traditions

by
Robin A. Leaver
Incumbent of St. Mary's Church, Castle Street, Reading

GROVE BOOKS
BRAMCOTE NOTTS

CONTENTS

ML
3166
.L4

THE FRONT COVER

The illustration on the front cover shows the titlepage block which appears in *Syntagma Musicum* (3 vols. Wittenberg and Wolfenboettel, 1614/15-1620) and *Musae Sionae* (9 vols. Magdeburg, 1605-1610). Both works were by Michael Praetorius (1571-1621), a composer and music scholar who eventually became Capellmeister to the Duke of Brunswick in Wolfenbeuttel. Praetorius, the son, grandson and brother of Lutheran pastors, offered an encyclopaedic survey of music in his *Syntagma Musicum* in which special consideration is given to the place of music in the worship of the Church, indeed, the first volume is virtually a history of church music. In *Musae Sionae* Praetorius collected together, edited, arranged and harmonized 537 hymn melodies in no less than 1,248 different settings. This valuable collection has not only been a witness to the hymns and melodies in use in the church of Praetorius' day, but has also provided a valuable source for later generations to draw from. The basic Lutheran hymn book today, *Evangelishes Kirchengesangbuch* (1950), contains five melodies written or adapted by Praetorius, and thirteen further settings are based on those found in *Musae Sionae*. In the hymnody of the Church of England Praetorius is known for his adaptation and harmonization of the melody *Es ist ein' Ros' entsprugenn (Anglican Hymn Book,* 90), and for the melody *Fuer deine empfangen Speis und Trank (English Hymnal,* 549).

The detail of the woodcut is worth careful scrutiny for there is a wealth of symbolism to be discovered. For example, the three vocal and instrumental groups of the music of the church on earth anticipate the antiphonal vocal and instrumental music of heaven, and both the music of earth and the music of heaven are directed toward the Lamb.

First Impression June 1976

ISSN 0306 0608

ISBN 0 901710 93 8

1. THE EARLY ENGLISH LITURGIES AND MUSIC

The musical resources for the un-reformed Mass in England were rich and magnificent. Examples of this heritage are to be found in the Old Hall and Egerton manuscripts as well as in the great choir books of Lambeth, Cambridge and Eton. When the reforming movement was little more than a clandestine religious study group, meeting in the White Horse Inn in Cambridge, the Latin Mass could be heard in the polyphonic settings of composers such as Robert Fayrfax, Robert Carver, John Taverner, John Marbeck, and many others. Such music was performed not only in the cathedrals and large churches of major towns but also in places like the small Suffolk village of Stoke by Clare where there was a collegiate chapel that maintained a choir of eighteen men and boys, presided over by its Dean, Matthew Parker.[1] Parker later became the famous Elizabethan Archbishop of Canterbury, but by then the whole musical atmosphere in the English church was very much different. In 1572, towards the end of Parker's archiepiscopate, a John Bossewell complained: 'But what saie I, Musicke? One of the seven Liberall sciences? It is almost banished this Realme.'[2]

This change in English church music came about largely for theological reasons. The Reformers had rediscovered the significance of the Scriptures as the rule and norm for faith and life. For example, in 1537 Myles Coverdale published his translation of Luther's commentary on Psalm 23. Alongside Luther's treatment of the second verse Coverdale adds the marginal comment: 'The chiefest good upon earth is to have God's word.'[3] If Scripture is thus 'the chiefest good' then men need to hear it, the Reformers reasoned, but in so much of the polyphonic church music of the day, though the sounds were truly magnificent, the one thing that was most difficult to hear was the verbal content of the text. As early as 1519 Erasmus had complained that 'modern church music is so constructed that the congregation cannot hear one distinct word.'[4] The Reformers began to demand that if music was to be a servant of the Word, then it should be written in a simpler style, preferably with only one note for each syllable. Such was Cranmer's recommendation to Henry VIII[5], and it is known that there were at least two sets of Injunctions—one to Lincoln Cathedral in 1548 and the other to York Minster in 1552[6]—requesting that this policy should be put into practice. Undoubtedly there would have been other such recommendations.

[1] See P. Le Huray, *Music and the Reformation in England 1549-1660*, (Jenkins, London, 1967) p.13.

[2] John Bossewell, *Workes of armorie, devyded into three bookes* (London, 1572), quoted by D. Stevens, *Tudor Church Music* (Faber, London, 1961) p.11.

[3] *Remains of Myles Coverdale*, ed., G. Pearson (Parker Society, Cambridge, 1846) p.297.

[4] *Paraphrasis in duas epistolas Pauli ad Corinthios* (Basle, 1519) commenting on 1 Corinthians 14.19, quoted in Le Huray, *op. cit.,* p.11; see C. A. Miller, 'Erasmus on Music', *The Musical Quarterly*, Vol. 52 (July, 1966), pp.332-49.

[5] The date of the letter is problematical but was probably written in 1544; *Miscellaneous Writings and Letters of Thomas Cranmer*, ed., J. Cox (Parker Society, Cambridge, 1846) p.412.

[6] Le Huray, *op. cit.,* pp.9 and 25.

However, music was given an important role in the new, reformed vernacular services. When in 1544 Cranmer issued his *Letanie with suffrages*, it was printed with simple melodies after the manner of plainsong,[1] which were sung in simple four-part settings.[2] Four years later *The Order of The Communion* was authorized and from the Wanley part-books it is known that in at least one church or chapel it was celebrated as a musical service. The same source reveals that the 1549 Prayer Book service of Communion was also regarded as a musical service.[3]

This conviction is confirmed by the existence of John Marbeck's *The booke of Common praier noted*, 1550,[4] and by the rubrics of the 1549 Prayer Book. The rubrics for the Communion service direct that the clerks, that is, the choir, sing in English the Introit, ninefold Kyrie, Gloria in excelsis Deo, Offertory Sentences, Sanctus, Agnus Dei, and the post-communion Sentences. The service seems to have been conceived of as essentially a dialogue between priest and clerks or a monologue by the priest[5], with the congregation indicating its participation and assent in the 'Amens', the ascription 'Glory be to Thee, O Lord' before the reading of the Gospel, and responses. This limited participation by the people was non-musical, apart from singing the 'Amens'. The opportunity was for the people to join with the clerks in singing the 'Amens' but one suspects that at this point in time the congregations were content to let the clerks answer for them. It is significant that the only place where a rubric directs the people to join with the clerks is in the ascription 'Glory be to Thee, O Lord', and that in Marbeck this ascription is not set to music. This concept of a limited role by the congregation at large is confirmed by Cranmer's reply to the Devon rebels in 1549. He explains that everything in public worship 'should be the act of the people and pertain to the people. And it standeth to reason that the priest should speak for you, and in your name, and you answer him again in your own person... The priest prayeth for you, and you answer *Amen* . . . The priest is your proctor and attorney to plead your cause, and to speak for you all.'[6] Thus the order of Communion in the

---

[1] This was included in *An exhortation unto praer, thought mete by the Kynges maiestie, and his clergye, to be read to the people* ... (Grafton, London, 1544). See J. E. Hunt, *Cranmer's First Litany, 1544, and Merbecke's Book of Common Prayer Noted, 1550* (S.P.C.K., London, 1939) pp.65-120; R. Steele, *The Earliest English Music Printing* (Bibliographical Society, London, 1903), p.37 and facs. 9 and 19.

[2] Two anonymous settings of the Litany are to be found in the Wanley part-books Bodleian Library, Oxford, Ms. Mus. Sch. E. 420-422. For musical examples of these Litany settings see Stevens, *op. cit*, p.19 and E. H. Fellowes, *English Cathedral Music*, new (5th) ed. revised by J. A. Westrup (Methuen, London, 1969), pp.36f.

[3] Three of the complete Communion settings in the Wanley part-books date from before 1549; six use the 1549 words.

[4] Hunt, *op. cit.*, pp.121-256. See also my forthcoming volume on Marbeck's life, music and theology which is to be published in the near future in the Courtenay Library of Reformation Classics, Appleford.

[5] The rubric before the Kyries reads: *'the Priest shall say, or else the Clerks shall sing.'* The rubric after the blessing states that *'where there are no clerks, there the Priest shall say all things appointed here for them to sing.'*

[6] Cranmer, *op. cit.*, p.169f. These sentences occur in a section in which Cranmer is arguing for the use of the vernacular: if the people's *Amen* is to be real then they must understand the prayer the priest has spoken. See also note 3 on p.5.

reformed Prayer Book of 1549 is a musical service only where there is a suitable choir present which sings on behalf of the congregation, in much the same way as the priest prays on behalf of the people. When there is no choir the service is said, but whether it is said or sung the congregation's role is largely one of passive assent.[1] This is a remarkable fact when one considers the Reformers' theology and the sources and influences behind the 1549 Prayer Book. Against the particular priesthood enunciated by the Church of Rome, the Reformers declared the priesthood of all believers,[2] and one might have expected to have found the advocacy of a more active participation on the part of the congregation, expressing such a universal priesthood, in this reformed service.[3] Furthermore, reference to continental church orders as well as to various English influences that lay behind the 1549 Prayer Book will reveal that an opportunity for congregational participation was either unfortunately missed or deliberately sidestepped. This, of course, was the congregational hymn. Undoubtedly a basic problem was that of illiteracy. This is reflected in the fact that neither the continental church orders nor the English Prayer Book gave a great deal for the people to *say*. But it would seem that the framers of the continental orders appreciated more fully than their English counterparts the peculiar quality that music has for helping people to remember words.

If one examines the Sarum use of the daily offices and compares them with Cranmer's offices of Mattins and Evensong in the 1549 Prayer Book, then it becomes clear that the one element the Reformer has omitted to make use of in his reformed daily prayers is the office hymn.[4] This is a little surprising for Cranmer had recently been working on his reformed Latin

---

[1] It might be argued that the people had the opportunity to answer in the various responses, especially in the orders for Mattins and Evensong. In time they may well have responded but only if the service was said. By comparing with Marbeck one cannot help but draw the conclusion that the clerks sang on behalf of the congregation. In the order for Mattins a rubric directs: 'Then the Minister shall say the Creed'; at the same place in Marbeck there is the instruction: 'The Quere with the Priest. "I believe . . ." ' (Hunt, *op. cit.*, p.143). Thus the responses to the priest's words were likely to have been made by the clerks alone, 'in the name of people.' Compare the rubrics before the general confession, the prayer of humble access, and before the prayer of thanksgiving after communion in the 1549 Holy Communion.

[2] See the passage from Cranmer quoted on p.4 opposite; *The Examination and Writings of John Philpot*, ed., R. Eden (Parker Society, Cambridge, 1842) p.406; *The Works of Roger Hutchinson*, ed., J. Bruce (Parker Society, Cambridge, 1842) p.50.

[3] Bucer, in his *Censura*, criticised the 1549 Prayer Book on this particular point. He writes: 'While the sacred prayers are being said in the name of the whole people, they should not only listen to the prayers with the greatest attention but they should also reply to the minister: and not only *Amen* but also those other things customarily said in reply to ministers . . . For these responses are not the concern of the clergy only . . . but of the whole people. It would therefore be suitable if the people were to recite with the minister, both the confession of sins and that prayer before the reception of the sacraments, *We do not presume . . .*, together with the thanksgiving after the sacraments have been taken, or to follow him as he recites them.' E. C. Whitaker, *Martin Bucer and The Book of Common Prayer* (Mayhew-McCrimmon, Great Wakering, for Alcuin Club (No. 55), 1974), p.144.

[4] The comparison is conveniently laid out in tabular form in Le Huray, *op. cit.*, pp.20-21.

Breviary in which he was careful to include office hymns.[1] Admittedly this Latin work (which was never issued) was intended for the clergy and not for congregations at large. However, it does indicate that Cranmer had no basic objection to hymn singing. Furthermore, the reformed Breviary shows signs of having been influenced by continental sources,[2] which, with other such sources, also influenced the final shape and content of the 1549 Prayer Book. One of these other sources was the series of church orders of the German congregation in Strasbourg. Contact with Strasbourg can be seen in the fact that in 1539 Richard Taverner included a translation of some prayers by Wolfgang Capito at the end of his *An epitome of the psalms*.[3] Capito (or Koepfel) was a co-reformer with Bucer and the publisher of the Strasbourg church orders and hymnbooks.[4] The theological foundations for the series of church orders in Strasbourg were laid by Bucer in his *Grund und Ursach . . . der Neuerungen an dem Nachtmahl des Herren* (The Foundation and Reasons for Reforming the Lord's Supper), Strasbourg, 1524.[5] In this work Bucer gives a description of how the Lord's Supper was celebrated at that time.[6] It reveals that hymn-singing played an important part in the worship. Hymns were sung after confession and absolution, a metrical version of the ten commandments after the epistle, a metrical version of the creed after the Gospel, and a hymn during or after the communion.[7] The later Strasbourg church orders confirm and extend the use of hymn-singing within the liturgy,[8] indeed, it was the custom to

---

[1] J. W. Legg (ed.) *Cranmer's Liturgical Projects* (Henry Bradshaw Society (No. 50) London, 1915). Cranmer was working on this revision between c. 1538 and c. 1545; see C. H. Smyth, *Cranmer and the Reformation under Edward VI* (S.P.C.K., London, 1973) pp.74-77.

[2] Part I is indebted to various Lutheran orders and Part II owes much to Quignon's Breviary; see J. W. Legg, *op. cit.*, introduction, *passim*.

[3] Richard Taverner, *An epitome of the psalmes; with divers prayers translated* (Bankes, London, 1539). The translation of Capito's prayers was incorporated into *The King's Primer* of 1545.

[4] Capito was also a liturgical reformer in his own right, producing the church orders for Berne (1532) and Frankfurt (1535); he also wrote three hymns which were widely used in German-speaking areas, see P. Wackernagel, *Das Deutsche Kirchenlied von der Aeltesten Zeit bis zu Anfang des XVII Jahrhunderts*, Vol. III (Olms, Hildesheim, 1964) pp.731-33. Cranmer had a great respect for Capito. He personally presented a treatise of the latter to Henry VIII in 1537; see *Miscellaneous Writings and Letters of Thomas Cranmer*. (Parker Society, Cambridge, 1846), pp.340f.

[5] The document is given in full in *Dr Martin Luther's Saemmtliche Schriften*, ed. J. G. Walch, 2nd ed., Vol. XX (Concordia, St. Louis, 1890) cols. 352-439; among others, Capito's name is included at the end of the document indicating his full agreement with its contents.

[6] Luther, *op. cit.*, col. 406f.; translated in W. D. Maxwell, *An Outline of Christian Worship, Its Development and Forms* (O.U.P., London, 1960) pp.100f.—reprinted in G. J. Cuming, *A History of Anglican Liturgy* (Macmillan, London, 1969) pp.324f.

[7] This communion hymn was Luther's *Gott sei gelobet;* see Maxwell, *op. cit.*, p.96.

[8] These later orders are conveniently summarized in Maxwell, *op. cit.*, pp.101-111, and Cuming, *op. cit.*, pp.38ff.; for the place of the hymn in the Strasbourg church orders see W. Blankenburg, 'Der gottesdienstliche Liedgesang der Gemeinde,' in *Leiturgia. Handbuch des Evangelischen Gottesdienstes*, ed. K. F. Mueller and W. Blankenburg, Vol. IV: *Die Musik des Evangelischen Gottesdienstes* (Stauda, Kassel, 1961) esp. pp.635-639.

publish the liturgy with the hymnbook. The importance of congregational hymn-singing within the liturgy can be seen in the *Psalmen, gebett, und Kirchen-uebung* of 1533. After the liturgical portion of the book there are given the musical settings the prose Kyrie, Gloria, Alleluia and Creed. At the beginning of the hymnbook stand four hymns:

1 Creed: Wir glauben all in einen Gott (Luther)
2 Commandments: Dies sind die heil'gen zehn gebot (Luther)
3 Communion: Gott sei gelobet (Luther)
4 Magnificat: Mein seel erhebt den Herrn mein (Pollio).[1]

These four hymns form a section of liturgical hymns before the remainder of metrical psalms and other hymns.

Some of Strasbourg's customs and practices were introduced into England through Hermann von Wied's *Consultation.* Bucer had played the leading part in framing its liturgy. It first appeared in German in 1543; in Latin in 1545, and in English (from the Latin) in 1547, being reprinted with minor revisions the following year. Cranmer had his own copy of the Latin version and the German original, as well as the Latin, had had some currency in England before the English version was produced. Consequently it became a major source in the compilation of the first Prayer Book. In the service of the Lord's Supper[2] hymns are directed to be sung by the 'clerks' while the congregation is assembling for worship, then, when all are present, the whole congregation joins in 'a psalm in the Douch [i.e. German] tongue.' Prose versions of the Kyrie and Gloria are sung but there is a hymn after the Epistle. The Creed is also sung but it is not indicated whether it should be metrical or prose. At the communion two hymns are specifically mentioned: *Gott sei gelobet* and *Jesus Christus unser Heiland,* both by Luther.

But however influential these sources were on the 1549 Prayer Book none of their suggestions regarding congregational hymn-singing found a place within its pages. Certainly, English poetry was in an elementary stage; there was no folk-tradition, as there was in Germany, to draw on, and there was certainly no English Luther who could produce fine vernacular hymns. Cranmer confessed to Henry VIII that he lacked the ability to write hymns.[3] Brightman comments: 'the version of the *Veni Creator* in the Ordinal of 1550, if it is his, confirms his judgment, and if not, shows that his colleagues were as incapable as himself.'[4] However, it is an oversimplification to conclude that the omission of hymns from the 1549 Prayer Book rubrics 'was probably caused, not by any hostility to metrical hymns, but the difficulty of obtaining them in English.'[5] On the contrary, there may well have been a good deal of hostility.

1 P. Wackernagel, *Bibliographie zur Geschichte des deutschen Kirchenlieds im XVI Jahrhundert* (Olms, Hildesheim, 1961) p.124.
2 Given in Cuming, *op. cit.,* pp.334-357.
3 See note 5 on p.3.
4 F. E. Brightman, *The English Rite,* 2nd rev. ed. (Rivingtons, London, 1921), Vol. 1, p.lxxxiii.
5 *Ibid.*

Hymns and metrical psalms were by no means unknown in England at this time. The Primers had included a smattering of English hymns during Henry VIII's reign[1] and before 1538 Myles Coverdale had produced his *Goostly Psalmes and Spirituall Songes,* forty-one hymns mostly translated from German souces. In 1542 or 1543 Coverdale issued his synopsis and partial translation of the Danish church order, drawn up by Bugenhagen in 1537. Coverdale's declared purpose was to influence the authorities of the realm to follow this example and produce a similar church order for England.[2] Coverdale not only indicates that hymn-singing formed an important part of the worship but also went to some lengths to explain how the singing was organized in Denmark: 'At the quire door, beside the table of the Lord, stand two good sober singing men, which... begin a psalm; and all the people, both old and young, with one voice do sing with them, after such a fashion that every note answereth to a syllable, and every syllable to one note commonly, so that a man may well understand what they sing... They sing the Paternoster in their mother tongue...' Then before the sermon 'after that the two foresaid men... hath orderly begun, all the church followeth, and sing with one voice unto the Holy Ghost this song *Veni, sancte Spiritus &c,* or such other like it, in their mother tongue.'[3] Coverdale's hymnbook began with three such hymns to the Holy Spirit.[4]

Sometime in 1547 or 1548 Thomas Sternhold published his *Certayne Psalmes, chosen out of the Psalter of David and drawen into English metre* containing nineteen metrical psalms. A second edition appeared posthumously in 1549, enlarged to contain thirty-seven psalms. It was this edition which provided the basic corpus of metrical psalms used in later English psalters. Sternhold is described on the titlepage as 'grome of ye Kynge's Maiesties roobes' and it is said that the young prince Edward overheard the psalms being sung and had them repeated in his presence. The prefaces of both the 1549 edition of Sternhold's psalms and Christopher Tye's *The Actes of the Apostles, translated into Englyshe Metre* (1553) indicate that devotional hymns and metrical psalms had been very popular for some time in court circles.[5] In 1549 another psalter was published, the first complete metrical psalter in English: Robert Crowley's *Psalter of David newely translated into Englysh metre.*

It is true that none of these collections contained great poetry and these early examples of English hymns and metrical psalms may have been somewhat artless and lacking in grace, but some were quite tolerable in their expression of Christian devotion and piety that Cranmer could well

---

[1] C. C. Butterworth, *The English Primers (1529-1545), Their Publication and Connection with the English Bible and the Reformation in England* (University of Pennsylvania Press, Philadelphia, 1953) *passim.*

[2] *The order that the churche and congregation of Chryst in Denmark, and in many places, countries and cities of Germany doth use...,* in *Writings and Translations of Myles Coverdale,* ed. G. Pearson (Parker Society, Cambridge, 1844) pp.469f.

[3] *Ibid,* p.471.

[4] *Remains of Myles Coverdale,* ed. G. Pearson (Parker Society, Cambridge, 1846) pp.541-543.

[5] Even Princess Elizabeth tried her hand at a metrical version of Psalm 14, written about 1548; *Select Poetry Chiefly Devotional of the Reign of Queen Elizabeth,* ed. E. Farr, Vol. 1 (Parker Society, Cambridge, 1845) p.1.

have used them if he had wanted to. The fact that he did not, together with the fact that he did not add a footnote somewhere in the Prayer Book explaining that when suitable English hymns became available they could be sung, seem to suggest that there may have been other reasons for Cranmer's silence on the matter. To be sure, there might have been antagonism on the part of the 'professional' singers to general congregational singing. When in 1559 metrical psalm-singing was introduced there were those in Exeter Cathedral, for example, who did their best to stop such congregational singing.[1] Later still the Gentlemen of the Chapel Royal thought it beneath them to join in the *ordinary* singing of metrical psalms with the congregation.[2]

What is of greater significance is the growth of Zwinglian views among an important group of English divines during the latter part of Henry VIII's reign. Contacts between England and Switzerland were frequent from the 1530's onwards, and much of the contact was with Zurich, the centre of Zwingli's reformation activities.[3] Zwingli, possibly the most musically gifted of all the sixteenth century reformers, took a very negative attitude toward the place of music in Christian worship.[4] By 1525 all music had been eliminated from services in Zurich and two years later Bullinger reported: 'Since they do not agree with the apostolic teaching the organs in the Great Minster in Zurich were broken up on the 9th of December in this year 1527. For from this time forth neither singing nor organs in the Church was wanted.'[5] Even though a number of hymnbooks were printed in Zurich from 1536/7 onwards they were not for use by the congregations of Zurich.[6] It was not until 1598 that vocal music was re-introduced into the worship of the Zurich churches.

Smyth reviews the Englishmen who visited Zurich from the 1530's and makes the following summary: 'The list of Englishmen at Zurich may be a short one, but it contained many distinguished names. The attitude of the Swiss towards them is fairly evident. They were generous with their hospitality, and anxious to convert their guests to Zwinglianism.'[7] Two English visitors to Zurich, William Turner and John Bale both published radical, bitterly polemical tracts, in 1543, which contain criticism of music along Erasmian/Zwinglian lines.[8] Both men, with others, were back in

[1] Le Huray, *op. cit.,* 375.

[2] *Ibid.,* p.71.

[3] See Smyth, *op. cit.,* chapter 3, *passim.*

[4] See C. Garside, *Zwingli and the Arts* (Yale U.P., New Haven and London, 1966) and the present writer's article on Zwingli in the forthcoming new edition of *Grove's Dictionary of Music and Musicians.*

[5] Quoted Garside, *op. cit.,* p.61.

[6] M. Jenny, *Geschichte des deutschen-schweizerischen evangelischen Gesangbuches im 16. Jahrhundert* (Baerenreiter, Basel, 1962); H. Reimann, *Die Einfuehrung des Kirchengesangs in der Zuercher Kirche nach der Reformation* (Zwingli-Verlag, Zurich, 1959).

[7] Smyth, *op. cit.,* p.94.

[8] William Turner, *The huntyng and fynding out of the Romyshe foxe . . .* (Basel, 1543); John Bale (under the pseudonym 'Johann Harryson'), *Yet a course at the Romyshe foxe . . .* (Zurich, 1543). This was issued as a sequel to Turner's tract. Turner's violent writings were subsequently banned and Bale's polemical obscenities earned him the name 'Bilious Bale.'

England by or soon after the accession of Edward VI and together must have constituted an important body of opinion and influence. It is quite likely that Cranmer was silent on the question of congregational hymns in the liturgy because of currency of Zwinglian views in the country: silence on the matter would serve to appease both conservative catholics who wanted to retain traditional ceremonial and music and also radical Zwinglians who wanted neither.

The success of the small but influential group of Zwinglians can be seen in the changes made for the 1552 Prayer Book. John Hooper, who had spent some time in Zurich, arrived back in England only a matter of weeks after the publication of the 1549 book. He wrote to Bullinger, Zwingli's successor: The book is 'very defective, and of doubtful construction, and, in some respects indeed, manifestly impious . . . I am so much offended with that book . . . that if it be not corrected, I neither can nor will communicate with the Church in the administration of the Supper . . .'[1] In 1550 Hooper was nominated to the see of Gloucester but his consecration was delayed on account of his refusal to wear the customary vestments and his desire not to be involved in 'supersticious ceremonies'. The ensuing vestment controversy[2] centring on the narrow issue of Hooper's protest against ceremonial in one particular service, is to be seen as a general protest against all ceremony and a demand for a basic and fundamental simplicity in liturgical forms. Music had been closely associated with ceremony and along with ceremonial practices music was condemned by these representatives of Zwingli in England. It is probably due to their influence and activity that at least two composers for the Latin rite, who sympathised with them, gave up composing altogether during the period of the introduction of the English rite.[3]

This being the climate, it is hardly surprising to find that the 1552 Prayer Book cancelled nearly all the provisions for singing and music in the 1549 Communion service.[4] There is no mention of the 'clerks' and the only place where singing is referred to is in connection with the *Gloria in excelsis Deo*, which now stands at the end of the service instead of its traditional place near the beginning. This single concession that the Gloria may be sung at the end of the service seems to imply that singing is something that is not really important to the liturgy and can easily be dispensed with.

The influence is from Zurich rather than Geneva. In 1550 appeared *The forme of common praiers used in the churches of Geneva . . . made by master Iohn Caluyne . . . translated out of the frenche into Englyshe. By William Huycke,* London: Whitchurch, 1550. This was a translation of Calvin's Genevan order of 1547, which owed much to the Strasbourg orders of Bucer. In this order metrical psalms and hymns are directed to

[1] 27 March 1550. *Original Letters Relative to the English Reformation,* ed. H. Robinson (Parker Society, Cambridge, 1846) Vol. 1 p.79.
[2] See Smyth, *op. cit.,* pp.202-220; C. Hopf, *Martin Bucer and the English Reformation,* (Blackwell, Oxford, 1946) pp.131-170.
[3] John Taverner and John Marbeck.
[4] A Zwinglian direction is perhaps hinted at in the final rubric of the 1549 Prayer Book. It directs that if a sermon is to be preached, then, among other things, the Litany, Gloria and Creed could be omitted, that is, the main musical parts of the service.

be sung after confession, before the blessing and also that the Creed could be sung.[1] Furthermore, another reformed church order reflecting the French Strasbourg orders was published in England the following year: *Liturgia sacra, seu ritus ministerii ecclesia peregrinorum propter Evangelium Christi Argentinae*, London: Stephen Mierdman, 1551.[2] In this order for the refugees in Glastonbury the singing of metrical hymns and psalms forms an important part of the liturgy. They are to be sung as part of the confession and after it, while the minister enters the pulpit, as a confession of faith (i.e. a metrical version of the Creed), and before the blessing.[3] A number of authorities, for example Proctor and Frere,[4] have drawn attention to this liturgy as the probable source for Cranmer's inclusion of the Ten Commandments at the beginning of the Communion service. Certainly the use of the Decalogue in the Communion service can be paralleled in many German church orders[5] but it is only in the Strasbourg usage, both French and German, that it forms part of the penitential introduction to the liturgy, and Poullain's *Liturgica sacra* presents the most developed use of the commandments at this juncture.

However, a point that is often overlooked is that Poullain directs that a metrical version of the commandments should be sung. From 1539 the French congregations in Strasbourg used Calvin's metrical version of the commandments,[6] which owes much to Luther's version *Dies sind die heil'gen zehn gebot,* which the German congregation in Strasbourg had been singing since 1525.[7] Both Luther and Calvin end each stanza with 'Kyrieleison'. However, in 1545 Calvin's version was displaced by Clement Marot's version, which was sung to the melody of Psalm 140 which was without the 'Kyrieleison'.[8] Poullain directs that the liturgy should begin with the singing of those verses which declare the first table of the Law. Then the people join in confessing their sin, appealing to God for mercy 'in the name of Jesus Christ our Lord', after which the minister reads sentences of Scripture declaring the assurance of forgiveness. Then follow the verses of the Decalogue hymn which deal with the second table of the Law, at the conclusion of which the minister prays that the Law should be 'written in their hearts through the Holy Spirit.' Finally, the last verse of the hymn is sung.[9]

1 See W. D. Maxwell, *The Liturgical Portions of the Genevan Service used by John Knox While Minister of the English Congregation of Marian Exiles at Geneva, 1556-1559* (Oliver and Boyd, Edinburgh and London, 1931) p.18.

2 Modern critical edition: A. C. Honders, *Valerandus Pollanus Liturgia Sacra (1551-1555)* (Brill, Leiden, 1970).

3 Honders, *op. cit.,* pp.54, 58, 60, 76.

4 F. Procter and W. H. Frere, *A New History of The Book of Common Prayer With a Rationale of its Offices* (Macmillan, London, 1905) pp.86f.

5 For examples, see C. Neil and J. M. Willoughby, *The Tutorial Prayer Book* (The Harrison Trust, London, 1912) p.298.

6 *Oyons la Loy que de sa voix;* R. R. Terry, *Calvin's First Psalter* (Benn, London, 1932) pp.57-60.

7 The two hymns have a similar metre and the same number of stanzas, but Calvin's is associated with a different melody.

8 *Lève le coeur, ouvre l'aureille;* P. Pidoux, *Le psautier huguenot* (Baerenreiter, Basel, 1962) Vol. 1, p.135.

9 Honders, *op. cit.,* pp.54f.; see also A. C. Honders, 'Let Us Confess Our Sins . . .', in *Concilium. Theology in the Age of Renewal,* new series, Vol. 2 (February, 1973), p.89.

The parallels with the 1552 Prayer Book liturgy are obvious. The Kyrie, 'Lord have mercy upon us', is repeated after each commandment and after the tenth commandment there is the added petition: 'and write all these Thy laws in our hearts.' But the differences are as great as important. In the Prayer Book order the commandments are not sung in metrical form nor is a distinction made between the two tables of the Law. If Cranmer was directly influenced by this liturgy of Poullain's, then, either for personal reasons or, more likely, from external pressures, he made no use of its hymnic prescriptions. This he could have done easily for Coverdale had included a translation of both Luther's hymns on the commandments in his *Goostly Psalmes*.[1]

Again one has to conclude that there must have been some hostility to music and singing to account for this silence on the matter of congregational hymns in the 1552 order which contrasts greatly at this point with the continental sources which influenced it. There was certainly a difference of opinion among Cranmer's advisers. Thomas Becon, Cranmer's chaplain, wrote his *The iewel of ioye* around the time the 1552 book was produced. In it he penned: 'There have been, (would God there were not now!) which have not spared to spend much riches in nourishing many idle singing men to bleat in their chapels . . . A Christian man's melody, after St. Paul's mind, consisteth in the heart, while we recite psalms, hymns and spiritual songs, and sing to the Lord in our hearts . . . All other outward melody is vain and transitory, and passeth away and cometh to nought. Vain and transitory it is indeed; notwithstanding, music may be used, so it be not abused. If it be soberly exercised and reputed as an handmaid unto virtue, it is tolerable; otherwise it is execrable and to be abhorred of all good men. So ye perceive that music is not so excellent a thing, that a Christian ought earnestly to rejoice in it.'[2] On the other hand, Martin Bucer, who had come to England as Cranmer's guest in 1548, had a far more positive regard for music. In his *Grund und Ursach* he declared: 'Paul wrote in Ephesians 5 that we should love God with all our might, why should we then not sing to Him also, as did the saints of the Old and New Testaments? as long as such singing is done from the heart; and this is what the Apostle means when he says, "and sing to the Lord from your hearts." For his meaning is not that we should sing without voice, for then it would be impossible for us to encourage and edify others, or how else could we speak with one another, concerning that which he writes to the Ephesians? Therefore, those who discard singing in the congregation of God know little, either about the contents of scripture or the custom of the first apostolic churches and congregations, who always praised God with singing . . .'[3] Later, in a preface to a Strasbourg hymnbook ssued in 1541, which was reprinted a number of times over the years, Bucer speaks of

---

[1] Coverdale, *Remains*, pp.544-546; both hymns conclude each stanza with 'kyrieleison'.
[2] *The Catechism of Thomas Becon, With Other Pieces Written by Him in the Reign of King Edward the Sixth* (Parker Society, Cambridge, 1844) p.429.
[3] Luther, *op. cit.*, col. 437. Trans. Ottomar Cyprys, whose complete translation of Bucer's *Grund und Ursach* is due for early publication in the Courtenay Library of Reformation Classics, Appleford.

music as 'this glorious art and gift of God' which is 'powerful beyond other things to stir up the soul and make it fervent and warm.'[1]

But the climate of opinion in England appears to have been against Bucer, which perhaps explains his failure to take up the question of congregational hymn-singing in his evaluation of the 1549 Prayer Book in his *Censura,* and also his comments on 'the regulation of ceremonies' in *De Regno Christi.* Here he states that the church in each country is free to define the content and scope of its liturgy—such as the administration of the sacraments, prayers, psalms, etc.—without outside interference, but adds: 'However, in any country or realm of the Church these thing may very conveniently be observed with as much conformity as possible, *not only for beauty's sake,* but also to engender a good opinion for Christian forms of worship.'[2] There may well be here a veiled exhortation to Englishmen to look at continental church orders, other than Zurich, and reflect on the fact that, whether Lutheran or Reformed, they all give important place to the music of congregational worship.

In his views on music Bucer was greatly influenced by Luther.[3] Had the opinions and practices of Wittenberg, mediated via Strasbourg, prevailed in England, rather than those of Zurich, then the revision of the Prayer Book which was issued in 1552 would have been significantly different.

---

[1] Wackernagel, *Bibliographie,* p.584; compare Bucer's un-puritan approach to music and dancing in his *De Regno Christi;* W. Pauck, ed., *Melanchthon and Bucer* (Library of Christian Classics, Vol. 19) (Westminster, Philadephia, 1969) pp.347ff.

[2] Pauck, *op. cit.,* p.256. Italics added.

[3] See W. E. Buszin, *Luther on Music* (Lutheran Society for Worship, Music and the Arts, St. Paul, 1958).

2. THE LUTHERAN LITURGICAL AND MUSICAL TRADITION

The influence of Lutheran church orders on the Edwardian Prayer Books was wide and varied.[1] Much of this influence came through Hermann von Wied's *Consultation*[2] of which Melanchthon as well as Bucer had had a part in the compilation. But it would be wrong to conclude that this was the only 'Lutheran' influence on the Prayer Books. Luther's writings and reforming activities had been widely known among the clergy of England for twenty years or more before the first Prayer Book was issued.[3] A certain amount of correspondence flowed between England and Germany and influential men such as Robert Barnes, John Rogers, Myles Coverdale, as well as Cranmer himself, had either studied or worked in Germany during this period. Thus it may be presumed that there was a significant 'oral tradition', as well as printed sources, that influenced the shape and content of the first Prayer Book. Such men would have experienced something of the variety of the German church orders as they travelled through the country. No doubt they recounted what they had seen and heard when they eventually returned to England. One of the strongest elements in these church orders was the place of the congregational hymn, the one element that was not taken up by the English Reformers, even though it had greatly influenced Bucer working in Strasbourg, and also, through him, Calvin in Strasbourg and later in Geneva. It is significant that Lutheran influences were strongest in the Prayer Book services of the Litany, Baptism and Marriage, and weakest—certainly in the 1552 Prayer Book—in the Holy Communion service. This undoubtedly reflects the eucharistic controversies of the time in which Englishmen took a Reformed rather than a Lutheran position. Indeed, as has been demonstrated earlier, a significant number took the radical Zwinglian view and held that in the liturgy of the Lord's Supper, the most solemn act of remembering the Lord, music and singing served only to distract. Such was the history; but it might have been different. It is informative to review the origins of congregational worship in Lutheranism, and its subsequent development with its important musical and liturgical elements, because it demonstrates that the English Reformers missed the opportunity for a practical expression of the priesthood of all believers in the liturgy.

Luther's first reformed liturgy was his *Formula Missae et Communionis pro Ecclesia Vuittembergensi* in 1523. In it he wrote: 'I wish that we had as

---

[1] See, for example, F. E. Brightman, *op. cit.*, Vol. 1, introduction and *passim;* H. E. Jacobs, *The Lutheran Movement in England During the Reigns of Henry VIII and Edward VI, and its Literary Movements* (rev. ed., Frederick, Philadelphia, 1892); L. D. Reed, *The Lutheran Liturgy* (rev. ed., Fortess, Philadelphia, 1959) pp.128-137.

[2] See C. Hopf, 'Lutheran Influences on the Baptismal Services of the Anglican Prayer Book of 1549,' in, *'And Other Pastors of Thy Flock': A German Tribute to the Bishop of Chichester,* ed., F. Hildebrandt (privately printed, Cambridge, 1942) pp.61-100. It was appropriate that this essay focusing attention on Hermann's *Consultation* should be in a collection of essays dedicated to a Bishop of Chichester for Cranmer's copy of the Latin edition of the work is preserved in the library of Chichester Cathedral.

[3] G. Rupp, *The Righteousness of God: Luther Studies* (Hodder, London, 1953) pp.37-42; N. S. Tjernagel, *Henry VIII and the Lutherans: A Study in Anglo-Lutheran Relations from 1521 to 1547* (Concordia, St. Louis, 1965).

many songs as possible in the vernacular which the people could sing during mass, immediately after the gradual and also after the Sanctus and Agnus Dei. For who doubts that originally all the people say these which now only the choir sings . . . But poets[1] are wanting among us, or not yet known, who could compose evangelical and spiritual songs, as St. Paul calls them, worthy to ve used in the church of God. In the meantime, one may sing after communion *Gott sei gelobet . . .* Another good (hymn) is *Nun bitten wir den Heiligen Geist* and also *Ein Kindelein so loebelich.* For few are found that are written in a proper devotional style. I mention this to encourage any German poets to compose evangelical hymns for us.'[2] Almost simultaneously with the *Formula Missae* there was published the first Lutheran hymnbook, the so-called *Acht Lieder Buch* (The Eight-Song-Book).[3] A German translation of the *Formula Missae* appeared in 1524 which contained an appendix of two further hymns,[4] and before the year was out the *Acht Lieder Buch* had been reprinted a number of times, two larger hymnbooks had been issued in Erfurt with reprints, and the influential *Geystliche gesangk Buchleyn* of Johann Walter had been published in Wittenberg, raising the repertory to thirty-two hymns.[5] This collection, which was reprinted many times and formed the basis for other collections, contains two of the communion hymns suggested by Luther for singing after communion, two metrical versions of the Creed,[6] and a number of hymns for the major festivals of the church year,[7] as well as a good selection of metrical psalms and general hymns.

Just over a year later Luther published his vernacular liturgy, *Deudsche Messe und ordnung Gottis dienstes,* Wittenberg, 1526. Here Luther directs that 'after the Epistle a German hymn, either *Nun bitten wir . . .,* or any other is sung with the whole choir,[8] and that 'after the Gospel the whole church sings the Creed in German: *Wir glauben all in Einen Gott.*'[9] 'The German Sanctus (i.e. *Iesaja dem Propheten* issued for the first time with the *Deutsche Messe*)or the hymn *Gott sei gelobet,* or the hymn of Johann Hus, *Jesus Christus unser Heiland,* could be sung . . . or the German Agnus Dei (i.e. *Christe, du Lamme Gottes*)'[10] at or after communion.

---

[1] Paul Speratus, who made a German translation of the *Formula Missae* the following year (1524), adds here: 'and musicians'; *Luthers Schriften* (St. Louis ed) Vol. X, col. 2252.

[2] *Luther's Works,* ed. J. Pelikan and H. T. Lehmann, Vol. 53: *Liturgy and Hymns,* ed. U. S. Leupold (Fortress, Philadelphia, 1965) pp.36f.

[3] See R. A. Leaver, 'A Decade of Hymns: Reflections on the Tenth Anniversary of the *Anglican Hymn Book' The Churchman,* Vol. 89 (April-June, 1975) pp.108f.

[4] See note 1 above and Wackernagel, *Bibliographie,* p.50.

[5] Of the 32 hymns in Walter's collection, 20 were translated by Coverdale in his *Goostly Psalmes.*

[6] Luther's *Wir glauben all in Einen Gott* and Speratus' *In Gott gelaub ich.*

[7] For example, *Nun komm der Heiden Heiland* (Advent), *Gelobet seistu Jesus Christ* (Christmas), *Christ lag in Todesbanden* (Easter), *Komm, heiliger Geist* (Whitsun), and *Gott der Vater wohn uns bei* (Trinity).

[8] *Luther's Works,* Vol. 53, p.74.

[9] *Ibid.,* p.78.

[10] *Ibid.,* pp.81f. See C. Mahrenholz, et al, *Handbuch zum Evangelischen Kirchengesangbuch,* Vol. III/1 (Evangelische Verlagsanstalt, Berlin, 1970) pp.482f.

The threefold Kyrie remains in its original language sung to simple plainsong, but the *Gloria in excelsis Deo* is strangely omitted. This clearly must have been an oversight. Luther had included it in the *Formula Missae*, which, he explained in the preface to the *Deutsche Messe*, he intended should be continued in those centres where Latin was understood. The *Gloria* continued to be used and a number of German versifications of it appeared, of which Decius' *Allein Gott in der Hoeh sei Ehr* came into almost universal use.

The important differences between the two liturgies is that whereas the *Formula Missae* directs that a vernacular hymn may be sung after the choir had sung settings of the prose Gloria, Creed, etc., the *Deutsche Messe* directs that German hymns, sung by both choir and congregation, should *replace* them. In time all the traditionally sung parts of the masse were available in German versifications which were used almost universally.[1] Thus it can be seen that right from the very beginning the Lutheran hymn or chorale[2] was considered as no general Christian song but as a vital part of the liturgy. Furthermore, the hymn presented the unique opportunity for the whole congregation to join together in the praise of God, both encouraging one another in their faith and demonstrating the doctrine of the priesthood of all believers in a practical way.

In the smaller towns and villages the *Deutsche Messe* formed the basis of the liturgy which was entirely in German. However, in the larger cities and university towns the liturgy was usually an amalgam of the *Formula Missae* and the *Deutsche Messe*. In these centres of education where Latin was the common language and the Kantorie tradition flourished,[3] it was customary for the choir to sing in Latin the Kyrie, Gloria, etc., if not on every Sunday at least on the major festivals of the church year. However, the singing of the Latin prose versions by the choir never replaced the singing of the congregation at large: the German metrical versions of the Gloria, Creed, etc., were always sung by the whole church together. This custom stands in marked contrast with the prescription of the first Edwardian Prayer Book which directs the clerks to sing on behalf of the general congregation, which, for the most part, remains silent.

A typical example of an order combining both Latin and German elements is that given in the *Hoch-Fuerstlichen Sachsen-Weissenfelsischen Vollstaendigen Gesang-und Kirchenbuch* of 1714.

---

[1] Kyrie—*Kyrie, Gott Vater in Ewigkeit;* Gloria—*Allein Gott in der Hoeh sei Ehr;* Creed— *Wir glauben all in Einen Gott;* Sanctus—*Jesaja dem Propheten;* Agnus Dei— *Christe, du Lamm Gottes.* For a summary of the place of the hymn within the Lutheran liturgy, see F. Blume, et al, *Protestant Church Music: A History* (Gollancz, London 1975) pp.63ff.

[2] 'Chorale' from 'choraliter' meaning 'sung in unison after the manner of plainsong.'

[3] Luther had no wish to destroy this choir-school tradition, and, suitably reformed, these medieval institutions continued to provide choral music for the liturgy of the Lutheran church. Lutheran Kantorei flourished in places such as Wittenberg, Torgau, Jena, Altenburg, Leipzig, etc., cf. J. Rautenstrauch, *Luther und die Pflege der Kirchlichen Musik in Sachsen,* (Olms, Hildesheim, 1970) pp.60-234.

LITURGY FOR ADVENT SUNDAY

1. Latin introit sung by the choir
2. Metrical version of Psalm 19 sung by whole congregation
3. Kyrie-Christe-Kyrie sung by the choir
4. Minister intones: *Gloria in excelsis Deo*
5. Choir continues: *Et in terra pax . . .*
6. The German Gloria: *Allein Gott in der Hoeh sei Ehr* sung by the whole congregation
7. Collect
8. Epistle
9. Congregational hymn: *Nun komm, der Heiden Heiland*
10. Gospel
11. 'Darauf ein Stueck musiciret,' i.e. the Cantata
12. The German Creed: *Wir glauben all in Einen Gott* sung by the whole congregation.[1]
13. Pulpit hymn: *Herr Jesu Christ, dich zu uns wend* sung by the whole congregation
14. Sermon
15. Second part of the Cantata
16. Congregation hymn: *Allein zu dir, Herr Jesu Christ*
17. Words of Institution
18. Communion, with communion hymns: *Jesus Christus unser Heiland* and others
19. Collects and Blessing
20. Congregational hymn: *Sei Lob und Ehr mit hohem Pries*[2]

It will be seen that a number of the congregational hymns answer and underline the singing of the choir. The important exception to this is the hymn which follows the reading of the Epistle. In the Roman rite this is where the gradual would be sung. In Luther's early days the gradual was a rather complicated gregorian dialogue between solo voice and choir. His reformed liturgies brought about a significant change in that the congregation at large, rather than the choir alone, took over the singing at this point in the liturgy.[3] In the Lutheran church orders of the sixteenth and seventeenth centuries this *gradual-hymn* became the chief hymn of the service. Standing between the Epistle and Gospel for the day its function was to expound the themes established by these lections. Hence it was sometimes referred to as the *de tempore* hymn, that is, the hymn appropriate for the time or season in the church year.[4] It also gave the congregation the opportunity to respond to the Epistle and prepare for the Gospel. In the *Geistliche lieder* (Wittenberg, 1533) there were ten gradual hymns for the church year; in Spangenberg's *Cantiones ecclesias . . . Kirchengesenge Deusch, auff die Sontage . . . durchs gantze Jar . . .* (Magdeburg, 1545)

---

[1] In many centres, Leipzig for example, it was customary to precede the *Wir glauben* with the choir singing the Latin: *Credo in unum Deum.*

[2] *Leiturgia*, Vol. IV, pp.631f. This Weissenfels order is one of a family of Saxon orders. Apart from the metrical psalm after the Introit and the provision of a place for the Cantata, the Weissenfels order is virtually that of the original order of Duke Henry of Saxony (Wittenberg, 1539/40), which in turn was based on Luther's *Deutsche Messe.*

[3] The Latin gradual continued for a time in Wittenberg but the emphasis was on the congregational hymn; see *Leiturgia*, Vol. IV, p.619.

[4] Latin *de tempore* hymns had been in use for some considerable time but they were associated more with the Breviary than the Missal. For the *de tempore* hymns associated with Sarum usage, see M. Frost, ed., *Historical Companion to Hymns Ancient and Modern* (Clowes, London, 1962) p.14.

there were about twenty; in the *Kirchen-Gesaeng* (Franckfurt, 1569) about thirty; and in Selnecker's *Christliche Psalmen, Lieder, und Kirchengesenge,* (Leipzig, 1587) there were forty-five, that is, approaching one hymn for each Sunday in the church year. Thus there grew up a hymn of the week plan, a basic corpus of hymns which put into musical/devotional form the main teachings of each Sunday in the church year, which also provided the basic raw material with which the composers of the classic period of Lutheranism worked. These hymns—both texts and melodies—provided inspiration for a wealth of organ, choral and instrumental music unequalled in any other branch of the Christian Church.

One may take as an example the music of J. S. Bach. Around the year 1714 he composed and compiled his collection of organ chorale preludes entitled *Orgelbuechlein.* The first major section of this collection amounts to a musical treatment of basic gradual hymns for the main Advent-Trinity section of the church year:

ADVENT		BWV[1]
1	Nun komm, der Heiden Heiland	599
2	Gottes Sohn ist kommen	600
3	Herr Christ, der ein'ge Gottes-Sohn	601
4	Lob sei dem almaechtigen Gott	602

CHRISTMAS		
5	Puer natus in Bethlehem	603
6	Lob sei Gott in des Himmels Thron	—
7	Gelobet seist du, Jesu Christ	604
8	Der Tag, der ist so freudenreich	605
9	Von Himmel hoch da komm ich her	606
10	Von Himmel kam der Engel Schaar	607
11	In dulci jubilo	608
12	Lobt Gott, ihr Christen, allzugleich	609
13	Jesu, meine Freude	610
14	Christum wir sollen loben schon	611
15	Wir Christenleut	612

NEW YEAR		
16	Helft mir Gott's Guete preisen	613
17	Das alte Jahr vergangen ist	614
18	In dir ist Freude	615

PURIFICATION[2]		
19	Mit Fried' und Freud' ich Fahr dahin	616
20	Herr Gott, nun schleus den Himmel	617

[1] BWV=*Thematisches-Verzeichnis der Musikalischen Werke von Johann Sebastian Bach* (Bach-Werke-Verzeichnis), ed. W. Schmieder (Breitkopf, Leipzig, 1966). The *Orgelbuechlein* exists only in manuscript form, indeed it remains incomplete. Thus where there is no BWV No. this indicates that although Bach planned to write a chorale prelude on the particular melody the piece was never composed—or at least, never written into the master copy.

[2] Bach appears to omit the Epiphany season. However, a comparison with, for example, Vopelius *Das Neu Leipziger Gesangbuch* (Leipzig, 1682) reveals that the specific hymns for the season are to be found either in Bach's Christmas (Nos. 5-15) or Catechism (Nos. 59-85) sections.

PASSION

21	O Lamm Gottes unschuldig	618
22	Christe, du Lamm Gottes	619
23	Christus, der uns selig macht	620
24	Da Jesus an dem Kreuze stund	621
25	O Mensch, bewein' dein' Suende gross	622
26	Wir danken dir, Herr Jesu Christ	623
27	Hilf Gott, das mir's gelinge	624
28	O Jesu, wie ist dein' Gestalt	—
29	O Traurigkeit, O Herzelied	—
30	Allein nach dir, Herr Jesu Christ	—
31	O wir armen Suender	—
32	Herzliebster Jesu, was hast du verbrochen	—
33	Nun giebt mein Jesus gute Nacht	—

EASTER

34	Christ lag in Todesbanden	625
35	Jesus Christus, unser Heiland, d. d.	626
36	Christ ist erstanden	627
37	Erstanden ist der heil'ge Christ	628
38	Erschienen ist der herrliche Tag	629
39	Heut' triumphiret Gottes Sohn	630

ASCENSION

40	Gen Himmel aufgefahren ist	—
41	Nun fruet euch, Gottes Kinder all	—

WHITSUN

42	Komm, heiliger Geist, erfuell	—
43	Komm, heiliger Geist, Herr Gott	—
44	Komm Gott, Schoepfer, heiliger Geist	631
45	Nun bitten wir den heil'gen Geist	—
46	Des heil'gen Geistes reiche Gnad	—
47	O heil'ger Geist, du goettlich's Feu'r	—
48	O heiliger Geist, O heiliger Gott	—

TRINITY

49	Herr Jesu Christ, dich zu uns wend	632
50	Leibster Jesu, wir sind hier	633-634
51	Gott der Vater, wohn uns bei	—
52	Allein Gott in der Hoeh' sei Ehr'	—
53	Der du bist Drei in Einigkeit	—

There follow five hymns for various festivals.

All the texts of these hymns, except nine (Nos. 13, 20, 28, 29, 32, 33, 48-50) originate in the classic sixteenth century period of hymn-writing which owed so much to Luther himself. All the nine exceptions date from approximately the mid-seventeenth century and were written by Crueger Franck, Rist, Herrmann and Clausnitzer. In other words, Bach did not include contemporary hymns[1] in this first major section of the *Orgelbuechlein,* which demonstrates the abiding value and use of this basic corpus

---

[1] By the time Bach was at work on the *Orgelbuechlein* the basic repertory of German hymns had run into many thousands. For example, the *Lueneburgisches Gesangbeuch* (1695) contained over 2,000 hymns, and the *Andaechtiger Seelen geistliches Brand- und Gantz-Opfer, Das ist, vollstaendiges Gesangbuch* (Leipzig, 1697) contained over 5,000! Bach later acted as musical editor for G. C. Schemelli's *Musicalisches Gesang-Buch* (Leipzig, 1736), a collection of nearly 1,000 hymns.

of important hymns sung Sunday by Sunday in Lutheran churches. Bach himself was greatly committed to the use of these traditional gradual hymns. When the Deacon of the Nicolaikirche in Leipzig attempted to use other hymns in 1728 Bach protested, pointing out that the custom was to use only hymns that were 'in accordance with the Gospels' as they were to be found in the Dresden *Gesangbuch*.[1] If one examines the total corpus of his church cantatas then it will readily be seen that in most of the cantatas the composer either has based the whole composition on the gradual hymn for the appropriate day, or else used it in some other way.[2]

If one examines the compositions of the long line of distinguished Lutheran composers from Luther to Bach[3] then it will be found that many of them were based on this collection of gradual hymns for the church year. However, there was no authoritative list of the hymns and there were variations reflecting the usage of different areas and different times,[4] but the majority of the hymns are to be found in most listings. Many of the compositions based on the hymns originated from the then current practice of antiphonal singing by choir and congregation, with organ or instrumental introductions and settings—the so-called *alternatims praxis*. 'Hymns were sung antiphonally by the unison-singing congregation and a 'partner'. The 'partner' was either a unison-singing choir (the *schola*), a choir singing in harmony (the *figural* choir), the organ playing an organ chorale such as the settings in Scheidt's *Das Goerlitzer Tabulaturbuch*, or a brass ensemble. Thus the congregation was usually busy every other stanza. When it was not singing, its 'partner' could bring into play the entire treasure of church music in order to unfold and interpret the melody, or *cantus firmus*, and thus interpret the content of the hymn to the congregation.'[5] In this way the unique ethos and treasury of Lutheran church music was built up over the years with the choir and/or instrumental resources—rather than competing with the congregation or merely adding a framework of beautiful sounds within which the liturgy was set—forming an integral part of the liturgy, stimulating and encouraging the total congregation in its collective proclamation of the Word through the hymn.

As the eighteenth century progressed, the gradual hymn declined in use and significance and in time disappeared altogether. Part of the problem was that the basic idea of a hymn of the week was too successful. Through-

1 H. T. David and A. Mendel, eds., *The Bach Reader: A Life of Johann Sebastian Bach in Letters and Documents*, rev. ed. (Dent, London, 1966) p.114; cf. C. Mahrenholz, 'Johann Sebastian Bach und der Gottesdienst seiner Zeit,' *Musik und Kirche*, Vol. 20 (1950), pp.145ff.

2 C. S. Terry, *Joh. Seb. Bach Cantata Texts, Sacred and Secular With a Reconstruction of the Leipzig Liturgy of His Period* (Holland, London, 1964). See esp. D. Gojowy, 'Lied und Sonntag in Gesangbuechern der Bach-Zeit. Zur Frage des "Detempore" bei Choraelen in Bachs Kantaten', *Bach-Jahrbuch*, 1972, pp.24-60.

3 E.g. Calvisius, Hassler, the various members of the Praetorius family, Schein, Vulpius, Tunder, and many more.

4 Compare, for example, the listing above of the hymn melodies included in the first section of Bach's *Orgelbeuchlein* (c.1714) with the first section of Samuel Scheidt's *Das Goerlitzer Tabulaturbuch* (1650); see Mahrenholz's edition: Peters 4494.

5 Paul Thomas, *The Hymn of the Week. Part I: Advent to Transfiguration* (Concordia, St. Louis, 1961) Foreword (no pagination). See further F. Blume, *Protestant Church Music*, pp.105f.

out the seventeenth century large numbers of hymnbooks were published and almost every one added more hymns to be used on each of the Sundays of the church year. The difference that a generation or so made can easily be demonstrated in a comparison of Schein's *Cantional* (Leipzig, 1645) with Vopelius' *Neu Leipziger Gesangbuch* (1682)[1]: the former has around 130 hymns designated for the Sundays in the church year; the latter around 230. Furthermore, towards the close of the century there were those, such as Johann Olearius, who wrote hymns on the whole series of Epistles and Gospels.[2] This availability of more hymns for each Sunday eventually led to the displacement of the traditional gradual hymns. Their eventual eclipse was completed by the forces of Pietism and Rationalism which brought with them a deep suspicion of liturgical forms and everything associated with them.

The hymn of the week plan was recovered in the Lutheran churches of Germany by the efforts of C. Mahrenholz and others at a time when the church was being threatened by the anti-Christian, Nazi nationalism of the 1930's. These men realized that the church would not be rescued by playing politics with the state but rather by a vigorous confession of the Christian Gospel.[3] Other pastors and musicians added their contributions and eventually the plan took root again within German Lutheranism and now forms the core of the *Evangelisches Kirchengesangbuch*,[4] which is the hymnbook used today by all the territorial churches in various parts of Germany, both East and West.

The first practical attempt at such a plan for American Lutheranism was apparently made by J. W. Doberstein who gave his own hymn of the week plan in his *The Minister's Prayer Book*,[5] which was planned to coincide with the publication of the new common hymn book for American Lutherans.[6] The interesting feature of this plan — which has been followed in this respect by every subsequent American plan — is that Doberstein did not simply take the hymns of the German plan and direct that they should be used in English translations. Certainly some translations from the German are used, but a great many in the plan are original English hymns.

In 1961 the Lutheran Church—Missouri Synod issued a hymn of the week plan to be used in conjunction with its own hymnbook.[7] In accordance with the traditional concept, the hymns were chosen to expound or

---

[1] J. Grimm, *Das Neu Leipziger Gesangbuch des Gottfried Vopelius* (Merseberger, Berlin, 1969) pp.291-299.

[2] Olearius' hymns were included in the *Neu-vermehrtes Hamburgisches Gesangbuch* (Hamburg, 1739 (1st ed., 1700)) Nos. 204-302.

[3] P. Reich, *Das Wochenlied* (Staudia, Kassel, 1952) pp.1ff.

[4] *Evangelishes Kirchengesangbuch* (Baerenreiter, Stammausgabe, Kassel, 1950). This is the basic edition to which each territorial church adds its own supplement. For the *Graduallied* assigned to each Sunday in the Church Year, see C. Mahrenholz, et al. *Handbuch zum Evangelischen Kirchengesangbuch*, Vol. I/1 (Evangelische Verlagsanstalt, Berlin, 1954) pp.224-239.

[5] J. W. Doberstein, *The Minister's Prayer Book. An Order of Prayers and Readings* (Collins, London, 1964 (1st ed., Muhlenberg, Philadelphia: 1959)) pp.61-125.

[6] *Service Book and Hymnal* (Augsburg, Minneapolis (on behalf of eight Lutheran church bodies), 1959).

[7] *The Lutheran Hymnal* (Concordia, St. Louis, 1941).

highlight the lections for each day. As the Lutheran Epistles and Gospels are virtually identical with those of the 1662 Prayer Book, it will be helpful to quote this listing in full:

Advent 1	Saviour of the nations, come*1
Advent 2	The Bridegroom soon will call us
Advent 3	Ye sons of men, O hearken
Advent 4	O come, O come, Emmanuel
Christmas Eve	All me heart this night rejoices
Christmas Day	All praise to Thee, Eternal God*
Christmas 1	To shepherds as they watched by night*
Circumcision	O blessed day when first was poured
Christmas 2	Thine honour save, O Christ, our Lord
Epiphany	How lovely shines the morning star
Epiphany 1	Of the Father's love begotten
Epiphany 2	Songs of thankfulness and praise
Epiphany 3	O Christ, our true and only Light
Epiphany 4	Seek where ye may to find a way
Epiphany 5	Lord Jesus Christ, with us abide
Transfiguration	How lovely shines the morning star
Septuagesima	Salvation unto us has come
Sexagesima	May God bestow on us His grace
Quinquagesima	Let us ever walk with Jesus
Lent 1	God the Father, be our stay*
Lent 2	When in the hour of utmost need
Lent 3	Lord of our life and God of our salvation
Lent 4	Jesus, priceless treasure*
Lent 5	The royal banners forward go
Palm Sunday	Ride on! Ride on in majesty
Maundy Thursday	Jesus Christ, our blessed Saviour*
Good Friday	A Lamb goes uncomplaining forth
Easter Day	Christ lay in death's strong bands*
Easter 1	Ye sons and daughters of the King
Easter 2	The King of love my Shepherd is
Easter 3	O little flock, fear not the foe
Easter 4	Dear Christians, one and all, rejoice*
Easter 5	Our Father, Thou in heaven above*
Ascension	On Christ's Ascension I now build
Ascension 1	If God had not been on our side
Pentecost	Come, Holy Ghost, God and Lord*
Trinity	Come, Holy Ghost, Creator blest*
Trinity 1	We now implore God the Holy Ghost*
Trinity 2	Awake, Thou Spirit, Who didst fire
Trinity 3	In Thee alone, O Christ, my Lord
Trinity 4	Creator Spirit, by Whose aid
Trinity 5	Come, follow Me, the Saviour spake
Trinity 6	All mankind fell in Adam's fall*
Trinity 7	All praise to God who reigns above
Trinity 8	O enter, Lord, Thy temple
Trinity 9	One thing's needful; Lord, this treasure
Trinity 10	Lord, to Thee I make confession
Trinity 11	From depths of woe I cry to Thee*

1 An asterisk marks those hymns which appear in Bach's list given above on pp.18-19.

Trinity 12	My soul, now bless Thy Maker
Trinity 13	Lord of glory, Who hast bought us
Trinity 14	From God shall nought divide me
Trinity 15	In God, my faithful God
Trinity 16	The Will of God is always best
Trinity 17	The Church's one foundation
Trinity 18	Lord, Thee I love with all my heart
S. Michael	Lord God, we all to Thee give praise
Trinity 19	Praise the Almighty, my soul
Trinity 20	O Lord, look down from heaven
Trinity 21	Lord, keep us steadfast in Thy Word
Trinity 22	O faithful God, thanks be to Thee
Trinity 23	In Thee, O Lord, have I put my trust
Reformation	Salvation unto us has come
Trinity 24	In the midst of earthly life
Trinity 25	Farewell, I gladly bid thee
Trinity 26	The Day is surely drawing near
Trinity 27	Wake, Awake, for night is flying

The plan was launched with a flood of helpful literature. Ralph D. Gehrke issued a useful article explaining the background and purpose of the plan in the *Concordia Theological Monthly*[1] in 1961, and during the following year the same journal carried notes on each of the hymns in its *Homiletics* section.[2] The Missouri-Synod's publishing house produced a series of practical booklets for pastors, organists and choir directors. First, there was a workbook by Ralph Gehrke[3] giving guidance on the main thrust of the teaching in the lections for each Sunday in the church year, which included guidance on how the hymn of the week could best be sung antiphonally by choir and congregation. Simultaneously there were published both a set of five books containing various choral settings of the hymns of the week, by composers of the past and of the present, for choirs to sing in alternation with their congregations[4]; and a set of organ pieces by one of the foremost church music composers of the day, to be used either as preludes or accompaniments to the antiphonal singing.[5]

However, in this modern revival of the hymn of the week plan the function of the hymn has been slightly changed. Traditionally it had been the

[1] R. D. Gehrke, 'The Hymn-of-the-Week Plan', *Concordia Theological Monthly*, Vol. 32 (November, 1961) pp.697-704. See also R. D. Gehrke, 'Selecting Hymns for the Service: Some Practical Suggestions', *Church Music 66.1* (St. Louis, 1966), pp.13-17, which compares the Missouri-Synod's hymn of the week plan with that drawn up by the Commission on Worship and Church Music of the American Lutheran Church.

[2] Compiled by R. Bergt and A. Klausmeier, *Concordia Theological Monthly*, Vol. 32 (1961), pp.705-14, 763-73; Vol. 33 (1962), pp.32-41, 96-105, 155-65, 229-36, 287-96, 350-61, 416-25, 484-96, 540-51, 605-616.

[3] R. D. Gehrke, *Planning the Service: A Workbook for Pastors, Organists and Choirmasters* (Concordia, St. Louis, 1961).

[4] Paul Thomas, *The Hymn of the Week*, Vols. 1-5 (Concordia, St. Louis, 1961).

[5] Jan Bender, *Tabulatura Americana. Pars Prima: The Hymn of the Week Organ Settings* (Op. 22) (Concordia, St. Louis, 1961). The title *Tabulatura* recollects Scheidt's *Das Goerlitzer Tabulaturbuch* of 1650.

gradual hymn, standing between the Epistle and Gospel, but in America the hymn of the week is sung after the Creed and before the sermon.[1] Formerly the hymn of the week was a response to the Epistle and a preparation for the Gospel; it is now a summary response to all the Scripture readings.

The basic Missouri-Synod plan has undergone a number of modifications in the light of the ongoing liturgical development of that church body. Of the sixty-seven hymns of the plan, sixteen were modified or changed in 1969 when the *Worship Supplement* was issued containing new liturgical forms and hymns.[2] In 1973 the Inter-Lutheran Commission on Worship issued *The Church Year Calendar and Lectionary* which introduced a three-year cycle of lections. As the hymn of the week plan was based on the traditional Epistles and Gospels, it clearly needed revision. This need has recently been met by Edward Klammer[3], who, perhaps, offers the best summary of this distinctive feature of Lutheran worship: 'With the substitution of a congregational hymn for the ancient gradual psalm the reformers created something entirely new. The congregational hymn was elevated to the same rank as the psalm in the Mass. While in the Mass the gradual psalm was intended as adoring meditation, the gradual hymn in the Lutheran mass had a much more complex character. It certainly was also intended as meditative adoration. But it was more than that. Just as the intrinsic character of all genuine church music is doxological proclamation, sung adoration, so also in the "singing and saying" through the text and melody of the gradual hymn, the good news of the Gospel is proclaimed in song.'[4]

---

1 In the modern liturgies the sermon precedes the Creed but the hymn of the week still follows the Creed.

2 *Worship Supplement* (Concordia, St. Louis, 1969) p.233. Of the sixteen, ten are changes and six are different versions (either new translations, new melodies or settings) of the prescribed hymns.

3 E. W. Klammer, 'A New Approach to the Hymn of the Week', *Church Music 75:1* (St. Louis, 1975) pp.23-25.

4 *Ibid.*, p.23.

3. MUSIC AND WORSHIP DURING THE FORMATIVE ELIZABETHAN PERIOD

The Anglican liturgical/musical tradition, though not without its unique features, is of a different order from that of the Lutheran tradition. The differences can be traced directly to the respective church orders of the sixteenth century. In Lutheran Germany the people's song was very much part of the liturgy and from this basic understanding the rich musical tradition developed. But in England liturgical/musical developments proceeded in another direction. If music was permitted in the liturgy then it was sung by a group of experts: the common man could only stand and listen. When eventually the hymn did take root in English soil, receiving official recognition, it was extra-liturgical. When the hymn was first used in Anglican worship it was as a pious, devotional song which was sung outside the Prayer Book offices.

Edward VI's reign was considerably shorter than it was hoped. The 1552 Prayer Book was hardly a year old when the young King died and the new Queen Mary began a systematic reversal of all the reforms that had taken place: the Latin Mass was restored with all the customs, ceremonies and music associated with it. Two alternatives faced England's protestants: either to remain and risk almost certain martyrdom, or to leave the country in the hope that Mary's reign would be a short one and the Reformation could be reintroduced under her successor. Many died for their faith and many moved to the continent, but not to north Germany where Lutheranism was strong. Instead they went to south German cities, such as Frankfurt and Strasbourg, where Reformed influence was marked, or to the strongly Reformed centres of Geneva and Zurich. Consequently these exiles did not experience anything of the varied liturgical/musical developments that were emerging within Lutheranism. Instead they came into close contact with the metrical psalms of Marot and Beza, sung to the austere but stirring melodies composed or edited by Bourgeois and Franc. However, there was no unanimity among the exiles.

A group of English exiles, including William Whittingham, William Williams, and others, arrived in Frankfurt in 1554. They were given permission to worship in one of the churches there, provided that they agreed with the doctrines of the French church and used its liturgy. This liturgy was none other than the one Poullain had published while he was in England.[1] Poullain had moved to Frankfurt some time before and appears to have been the superintendent of the French congregation. The English congregation appointed two ministers: John Knox and Thomas Lever (or Leaver). During the ensuing months other exiles came to join them. A division quickly developed among them over the question of liturgical worship: one party wanted the Reformed liturgy of Poullain, or perhaps the English translation of Calvin's Genevan order, and the other group wanted to use the 1552 Prayer Book.[2] A compromise solution drawn

---

[1] *Liturgia sacra, seu ritus Ministerii in Ecclesia peregrinorum Francofordiae od Moenum* (Frankfurt, 1554). It was reprinted the following year; cf. A. C. Honders, *Liturgia Sacra*, p.6.

[2] The unfortunate affair is described in *A Brieff discours off the troubles begonne at Franckford in Germany Anno Domini, 1554 . . .* (reprinted, Petheram, London, 1846).

up by Lever failed and the English congregation was completely split down the middle, with Lever and Richard Cox (who had been involved in the production of both Edwardian Prayer Books) leading the Prayer Book party, and Knox and Whittingham leading the Reformed party. In the end the Reformed party were out-voted, which left them no alternative but to move on to Geneva.

As soon as they arrived in Geneva Knox began work on an English Reformed liturgy[1] and Whittingham on an English metrical psalter.[2] The fruits of their labours were published in a single volume, issued in Geneva in 1556. Congregational singing was thus encouraged within the *Sunday Morning Service* of the English exiles in Geneva. For example, after the rather lengthy exhortation and confession a rubric directs: 'This done, the people singe a Psalm all together, in a playne tune.'[3]

The death of Queen Mary in November 1558 and the accession of Elizabeth was the signal for the exiles to return to their home country. With them they brought their copies of *The Forme of Prayer,* which included the metrical psalter. It was, perhaps, the influence of this psalter that led to Elizabeth including the first official sanction of hymn-singing in the reformed Church of England in her Injunctions of 1559: '. . . for the comforting of such that delight in music, it may be permitted that in the beginning, or in the end of common prayers, either at morning or evening, there may be sung a hymn, or such like song, to the praise of Almighty God, in the best sort of melody and music that may be conveniently devised, having respect that the sentence of the hymn may be understood and perceived.'[4] Although permission was given for the singing of hymns, they were not to interrupt the liturgy and could only be used before or after the prescribed Prayer Book services, which were then available in the 1559 Prayer Book, being a moderately modified version of the 1552 book. But the introduction of this psalm-singing was not without its problems. There were troubles at Exeter Cathedral which prompted Lord Montjoye to write to the Dean and Chapter, on December 16, 1559, saying: '. . . whereas in the queen's majesty's late visitation . . . order was taken, that the vicars of your church should weekly . . . say the morning prayer in the choir of your cathedral church, whereunto the people might . . . meet together to serve God; and they so resorting reverently, and in great numbers . . . appointed among themselves at every such meeting to sing a psalm, and altogether with one voice to give praise unto God . . . which order, taken by the visitors, you promised by your corporal oath to see observed. We have now of late heard say, that contrary to the said order, and your own oath, certain of your vicars have scoffed and jested openly at the godly doings of the people on this behalf, and by divers and sundry ways have molested and troubled them; and that you the canons there . . . have very discourteously forbidden them the use of your choir [that is, the area of the

---

1 See W. D. Maxwell, *The Liturgical Portion of the Genevan Service Book Used by John Knox While Minister of the English Congregation of Marian Exiles at Geneva, 1556-1559* (Oliver & Boyd, Edinburgh and London, 1931).

2 M. Frost, *English and Scottish Psalm and Hymn Tunes c.1543-1677* (S.P.C.K., London, 1953) p.3.

3 Maxwell, *Genevan Service Book,* p.88.

4 Quoted Le Huray, *op. cit.,* p.33.

Cathedral and not the singers!] . . .'[1] Remembering that it was in Devon that there was hostility to the 1549 Prayer Book, this opposition might well have been another example of Catholic reaction. However, the reason might have been more significant. The incident occurred in late 1559, that is, before the first Elizabethan metrical psalter had been published. Thus, unless this large congregation sang from memory, copies of the Anglo-Genevan psalter must have been used. Two editions of this book had been published by this date (1556 and 1558) and both had been issued as part of Knox's *The Forme of Prayers and Ministration of the Sacraments, &c., used in the Englyshe Congregation at Geneva: and approved, by the famous and Godly learned man, Iohn Calvin.*[2] The opposition at Exeter could well have been more a protest against the *Forme of Prayers* rather than a protest against the singing of metrical psalms. It could have been interpreted as an attempt to displace the Prayer Book in favour of the Genevan order, recalling the division between the Prayer Book and puritan parties among the English exiles in Frankfurt some five years earlier. That this was the reason for the troubles at Exeter seems to be confirmed by the issue of the Elizabethan psalter the following year (1560): *Psalmes of David in Englishe metre, by Thomas Sterneholde and others . . . Newly set forth and allowed, according to the order appointed in the Quenes Maiesties Iniunctions.*[3] This psalter was a revision of the Anglo-Genevan Psalter of 1558 with a number of notable additions. These additions confirm its intended 'Anglican' use in that they provide metrical versions of some of the canticles. Nor is it without significance that the sole surviving copy of the psalter at Christ Church, Oxford, is bound up with a 1560 imprint of the Prayer Book. It is worthy of note that these revisions and changes from the Anglo-Genevan psalter of 1558 display Lutheran influences. In particular the 1560/61 English psalters introduced five German hymns with their melodies:

1 *God be merciful unto us* (Ps. 67) translated by Robert Wisdom from Luther's *Es wollt uns Gott genaedig.*

2 *Those that do put their confidence* (Ps. 125) translated by Wisdom from the anonymous *Nun welche hie ihr Hoffnung.*

3 *Our Father which in heaven art* translated by Richard Cox from Luther's *Vater unser im Himmelreich*

4 *Preserve us Lord by Thy dear Word,* translated by Wisdom from Luther's *Erhalt uns bei deinem Wort.*

5 *Give peace in these our days,* translated by Edmund Grindal from Capito's *Gib Fried zu unser Zeit, O Herr.*

All three of the translators were staunch 'Prayer Book' men. Both Cox and Wisdom were in Frankfurt during the problems of 1554 and sided against Knox and Whittingham. Grindal, later Archbishop of Canterbury, had been a friend of Bucer and took a similar moderate line.[4] All three translators were exiles during Mary's reign, but in Strasbourg rather than Geneva. All five hymns have associations with Strasbourg *Gesangbucher*. The first to

---

[1] Quoted, *ibid.,* pp.375f.

[2] Frost, *Psalm and Hymn Tunes,* pp.3-4.

[3] *Ibid.,* pp.5-8.

[4] Grindal was instrumental in arranging for Bucer's *Censura* and other writings to be published by Conrad Huber in 1577; cf. W. Pauck, ed., *Melanchthon and Bucer* (The Library of Christian Classics, Vol. 19) (Westminster, Philadelphia, 1969) p.172.

include all five hymns was *Ein New Auserlesen Gesangbeuchlein* ... (with a preface by Bucer), Strasbourg, 1545[1]; it was reprinted in 1547 and formed the basis of the new edition of 1559. It is highly likely that the English translators used the 1547 reprint.

However, this Lutheran influence was extremely limited and concerned only these hymns and not the strong musical tradition that was then being established in Germany. Indeed, both Grindal and Wisdom were later to register their opposition to the use of organs in churches. Furthermore, even though they were prepared to take some hymns from the Strasbourg *Gesangbuch,* they did not insist that they should be sung within the liturgy as in Strasbourg—or even Geneva for that matter!

The new psalm-singing was popular. John Jewel wrote to Peter Martyr on March 5, 1560: 'The practice of joining in church music (i.e., metrical psalms) has very muched helped ... For as soon as they had once begun singing in public, in only one little church in London, immediately not only in the churches in the neighbourhood, but even in the towns far distant began to vie with each other in the same practice. You may now sometimes sometimes see at St. Paul's Cross *after the service,* six thousand persons, old and young, of both sexes, all singing together and praising God.'[2] Significantly the psalm-singing took place *after the service,* confirming the instructions of the Injunctions of 1559 that hymns could be sung 'in the beginning, or in the end of common prayers,' which also appears to have been the practice of the psalm-singing Devonians of Exeter. The impression one gains is that at this early period the psalm-singing took place while the people were assembling for worship, or after it had been completed, but not during the liturgy. The printer John Day, who held the license to print 'the Psalmes in meeter, with Notes to singe them in the Churches, as well as in foure parts as in playne songe,'[3] simply mentions on his titlepages before 1566 that these psalms were 'allowed according to the Quenes Maiesties Iniunctions,' that is, before or after the service. From 1566 Day altered the wording of his titlepages to read: 'allowed to bee soong of the people together, in Churches, before and after Morning and Evening prayer: as also before and after the Sermon.'[4] Here the indication is that the metrical psalm had been given a limited place within the liturgy. However, one must remember that sermons were something of a rarity in Elizabethan England and often when they were preached they took place after the liturgy had been concluded, and sometimes at another venue, such as the examples at St. Paul's Cross referred to above. Although it is possible to see the beginnings of hymn-singing fulfilling a liturgical function within the English Church, it was a far cry from the vigorous liturgical hymn-singing of the German-speaking Churches on the continent.

[1] Wackernagel, *Bibliographie,* p.201; Bucer's preface is given in full on pp.584-5.

[2] Italics added: *Zurich Letters,* ed. H. Robinson (Parker Society, Cambridge, 1852) Vol. 1, p.71. Perhaps the occasion was Grindall's first public sermon as Bishop of London at St. Paul's Cross; see Le Huray, *op. cit.,* p.374.

[3] R. Steele, *The Earliest English Music Printing* (Bibliographical Society, London, 1903) p.13.

[4] *Ibid.,* p.47.

4. BEYOND THE ANGLICAN STATUS QUO

From the Elizabethan period there developed the twin-strands of the Anglican musical tradition: the splendid tradition of English cathedral music which the congregation at large listened to but never participated in; and the parish church tradition in which the metrical psalm effectively became the people's song.[1]

The choral foundation of cathedrals and collegiate bodies, albeit with some difficulty, continued to function during Elizabethan times. By about 1580 they became firmly established and from this time many more composers produced settings of the Prayer Book services, and, apart from the set-back of the commonwealth period, they have continued to function in their own distinctive way down to the present day.

The parish church tradition of metrical psalm-singing was the staple musical diet for Church of England congregations for approaching three-hundred years. Indeed, the influence was so strong that the metrical psalm was most probably the original inspiration for the verse anthem, a distinctive feature of English cathedral music.[2] For a hundred years or more the *Old Version* of Sternhold and Hopkins was the psalter in almost universal use, though not without criticism of some of the doggerel that passed for poetry.[3] In 1696 the *New Version* of Tate and Brady appeared and it eventually displaced the *Old Version,* although some parishes tenaciously hung on to their Sternhold and Hopkins until quite late in the eighteenth century. Similarly, the *New Version* in some parishes was still being used in the mid-nineteenth century and even later. However, largely as a result of the Evangelical movement within the Church of England, a new development occurred in psalm-singing. Instead of singing either the *Old Version* or the *New Version,* composite volumes were issued with the psalms taken from both versions as well as from Watts' *The Psalms of David* (London, 1719), to which a selection of hymns were added. The most influential of these were Madan's[4] and Topady's[5] and in time many towns and parishes provided their own collections.[6] It is interesting to note that these collections were invariably called *Psalms and Hymns,* whereas the titlepages of the earlier Lutheran hymnbooks were generally the other way round: *Hymns and Psalms.* This difference in titlepage reflects a difference in the understanding of the function of hymn-singing in worship. In England hymns were sung *at* the liturgy whereas in Germany they were sung *as part of* the liturgy, and therefore, these hymns had priority over the metrical psalms which had a less specific liturgical content.

[1] The question of how widespread was the singing of the prose psalter in parish churches requires a separate study, but it appears that before the nineteenth century such chanting was confined to cathedrals and similar bodies.

[2] Le Huray, *op. cit.,* p.217.

[3] For example, the oft-quoted complaint of the Earl of Rochester; J. Julian, *A Dictionary of Hymnology* (rev. ed., Murray, London, 1915) p.865.

[4] M. Madan, *A Collection of Psalms and Hymns* (London, 1760).

[5] A. M. Toplady, *Psalms and Hymns for Public and Private Worship* (London, 1776).

[6] For example, various congregations in Reading, Berks, used, among others: W. B. Cadogan, *Psalms and Hymns* (London, 1797); H. Gauntlett, *A Selection of Psalms and Hymns* (Reading, 1807) R. Binfield, *Select Psalms and Hymns* (Reading, 1809).

The change from basic metrical psalms to general hymns attuned to liturgical needs in English parishes is attributable to the influence of the Tractarian and subsequent Anglo-Catholic movements within the Church of England. The Tractarians were driven by the practical necessities of their aims to reconsider the place of music in worship and especially the use of hymns. Around the mid-nineteenth century a number of Tractarian hymn-books appeared, preparing the way for *Hymns Ancient and Modern* (1860), which has dominated Anglican hymn-singing ever since. Thus liturgical hymns were admitted into the worship of the Church of England, even though many of them were theologically alien to the Reformation principles which had created the Anglican liturgy and made it what it was.

The Tractarians were also in large measure responsible for the choral revival of the nineteenth century in which the cathedral music tradition was adapted and introduced into parish churches. This necessitated structural alterations such as the enlargement of chancels to accommodate surpliced choirs, who, like their cathedral counterparts, sang on behalf of the congregation, which could only listen and wait its turn to join in a hymn. In the old psalm-singing days, being led by the parish clerk and accompanied by the strange combination of clarinet, violin, double-bass and serpent may not have been musically satisfying but at least the whole congregation were together, demonstrating the unity of the people of God in their singing and playing. However, this unity was disturbed by the influence of Tractarian theology and practice which effectively divided the congregation into three: the priests and those who served them, the choir, and the remainder of the congregation. The choir being physically divided off from the general congregation, together with their different music, led to a feeling of superiority—that somehow their singing was more important than the *ordinary* hymn-singing of the congregation. This was the practical outcome of the choral revival in so many churches and even today there are parishes whose work and witness are being undermined by the 'them and us' syndrome of choirs and congregations.

The function of choirs and the role of congregational singing needs to be thought out afresh in the light of the liturgical experiments of recent years. For the first time in the history of Anglican liturgies the use of the hymn is specifically permitted in the rubrics of the new services.[1] Now there is the opportunity to involve both choir and congregation in a new approach to hymn-singing. In other words, we are now presented with the opportunity of drawing on the Lutheran emphases with regard to the place of music in the liturgy which were never taken up in the sixteenth century.

One of the strongest features of the sixteenth century Lutheran church orders is to be seen in the metrical alternatives to the *Gloria in Excelsis Deo, Creed,* etc.[2] I would venture to suggest that we need such metrical alter-

---

[1] I am ignoring the 'Come Holy Ghost' of the ordinal (which, incidentally, is not called a hymn in the preceding rubric). Even though the rubric after the third collect at Morning and Evening Prayer in the 1662 Prayer Book is generally accepted as allowing a hymn, it only speaks of an anthem: *'In Quires and Places where they sing here followeth the Anthem.'*

[2] Such metrical alternatives are in use in Roman Catholic Churches. See, for example, *Gottelsob: Katholisches Gebet- und Gesangbuch* (Katholischen Bibelanstalt, Stuttgart, 1975).

natives to use in our modern services. Admittedly, it may well be stimulating to sing the prose *Gloria*, etc., in the settings of John Rutter and others, but it is debatable whether they can become fixed in the minds and hearts of generations as did Decius' German Gloria *Allein Gott in der Hoeh sei Ehr* or Luther's German Creed *Wir glauben all in Einen Gott*. Furthermore, in the new series of Morning and Evening Prayer more canticles are provided. Would we not be doing our congregations a service if we gave them good metrical alternatives to sing?

Another feature of the Lutheran tradition is the *Alternatims praxis* where all the musical resources—congregation, choir, organ, and any other instruments—join in making music to the Lord together. For example, the hymn *O come, O come, Emmanuel* can effectively be sung antiphonally. In every other verse the congregation can sing the first four lines with the choir joining them in the last two lines: 'Rejoice! Rejoice! Emmanuel! shall come . . .' Then on the alternate verses the opposite procedure can be adopted: the choir sings the first four lines with the congregation joining them in the last two lines. In the preface to *The Hymn of the Week*, Paul Thomas makes the following suggestion regarding the hymn *Saviour of the nations, come*, which is Luther's version of *Veni redemptor omnium*, attributed to Ambrose:

Introduction:	Scheidt setting in *Das Goerlitzer Tabulaturbuch*[1]
Verse 1:	Congregation
Verse 2:	Choir[2]
Verse 3:	Congregation
Verse 4:	Choir[2]
Verse 5:	Congregation
Verse 6:	Choir in unison or a children's choir
Verse 7:	All. Organist uses Bender's setting.[3]

If instrumental resources are available—such as woodwind, brass, string, or recorder sections—they can join with the choir and substitute for the organ introduction. There is no reason why the final verse of the hymn treated in this way should not have its own organ or instrumental introduction. Any hymn can be sung according to this pattern, using whatever resources are available. Thus 'the congregation is drawn into the music-making of choir and organ, even as choir and organ by their subjection to the *cantus firmus* (melody) of the congregation's hymn show that they know that they are not called independently to lord it over the congregation but rather serve it in its worship.'[4] Also, if there is careful planning, the hymn melody itself can operate as a musical theme throughout the whole service.[5]

[1] Peters ed. p.1—two versions.
[2] In a setting by Vulpius, given in Thomas, *Hymn of the Week*, I, p.3.
[3] Bender, *Hymn of the Week Organ Settings*, p.4.
[4] R. D. Gehrke, 'The Hymn-of-the-Week Plan', p.701.
[5] See introduction to, R. A. Leaver, *A Thematic Guide to the Anglican Hymn Book* (Church Book Room Press, London, 1975). Two important sources of suitable material are: *A Vocal Companion to Bach's Orgelbuechlein*, ed. W. Emery, 3 Vols. (Novello, London, 1971-1975) which contain forty-five varied choral settings of the German
[continued overleaf

The third significant feature of the Lutheran tradition is the use of the gradual hymn—the hymn of the week—to be the main hymn of the liturgy, and to form part of the congregation's response to the reading of the Word. The Series 3 Communion service allows that between the Epistle and Gospel 'a canticle, a hymn, or a psalm may be sung.' If the proper psalm is used between the Old Testament lesson and the Epistle, there is the opportunity to introduce a gradual hymn, or hymn of the week, between the Epistle and Gospel. The two-year lectionary associated with Series 3 explores a rich series of themes Sunday by Sunday in which all three lections fit together thematically in a far more satisfactory way than the traditional Epistles and Gospels. The prospect of developing a hymn of the week plan is both exciting and daunting. Nevertheless it is one of the urgent needs of the church today. The present writer has drawn up such a plan using hymns from the *Anglican Hymn Book*,[1] but the real need is for a more radical approach using traditional as well as modern hymns, commissioning new hymns where they are needed. The traditional hymns would be chosen not only for their own sake but also with an eye to the choral, instrumental and organ compositions based on their melodies which could be used in antiphonal singing. With regard to newer hymns which have no such rich heritage, the need is to encourage contemporary composers to provide a variety of settings.

When Luther introduced his reformed liturgy in 1523 he was aware of a need: 'I wish we had as many hymns as possible . . . which the people could sing . . . (at) the gradual . . . But poets and musicians are wanting among us, or not yet known, who could compose evangelical and spiritual hymns . . . I mention this to encourage any . . . poets to compose evangelical hymns for us.'[2]

It would seem we have a similar need today.

Footnote 5 from p.31 continued]

> melodies; and *Hymns for Choirs arranged for mixed voices and organ,* ed. D. Willcocks (Oxford University Press, London, 1976) which is a kind of choral companion-volume to either *The English Hymnal* or *Hymns Ancient and Modern Revised* (though it can be used with other hymn books), and presents fifty texts of familiar hymns with twenty-nine settings of their associated melodies. They cover the main seasons and festivals of the church year, with the exception of Christmas as such settings are to be found in *Carols for Choirs,* ed. D. Willcocks, R. Jacques, and John Rutter, 2 vols. (Oxford University Press, London, 1961-1970).

[1] Leaver, *op. cit.,* pp.i-vii.
[2] See above pp.14f.